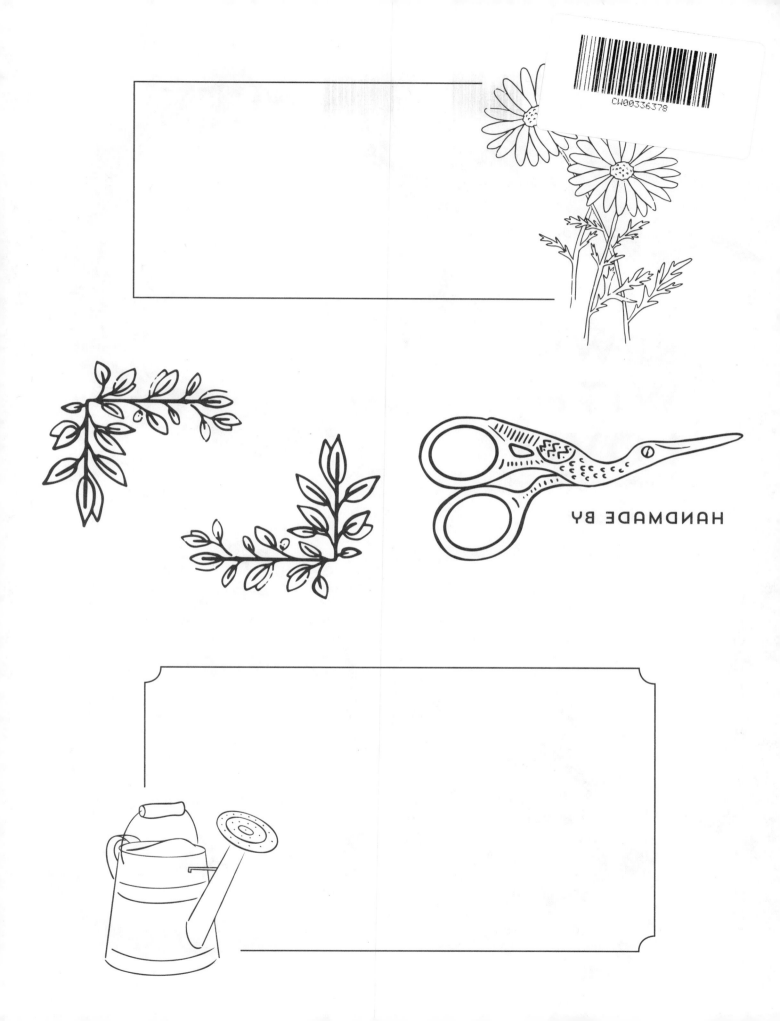

HANDMADE BY

SEWN
WITH
LOVE

Made Especially for You

SEWN
WITH
LOVE

Made Especially for You

HAND WASH ONLY

MACHINE WASH
COLD
GENTLE CYCLE

Date Started:

Date Finished:

made by:

date:

This quilt was made for cuddles.

for:
by:
date:

MADE WITH
LOVE

for:

by:

date:

MADE WITH

LOVE

MADE FOR:
DATE:

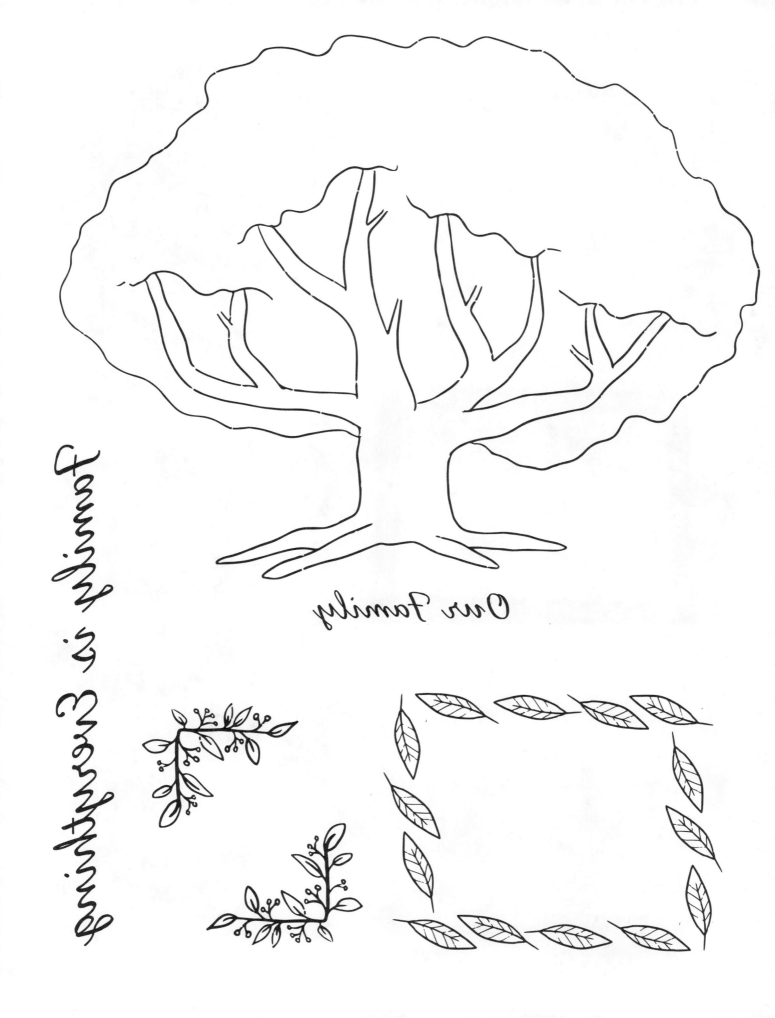

Our Family

Family is Everything

There is no
place like
home.

New Home
New Memories

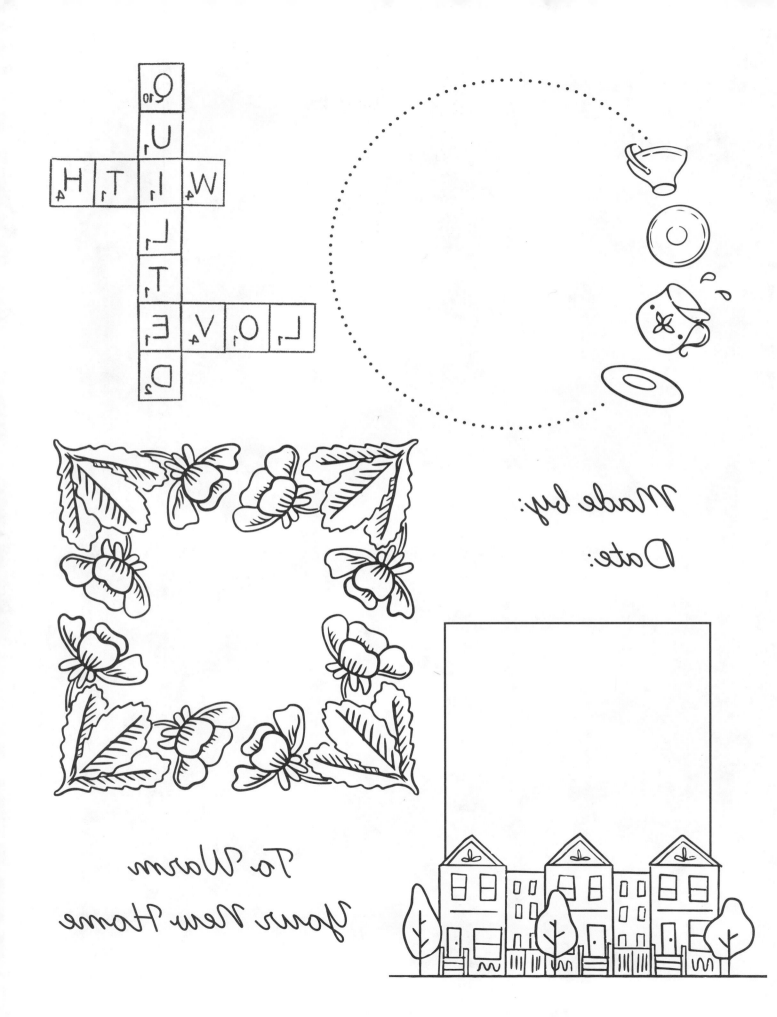

QUILTED WITH LOVE

Made by:

Date:

To Warm

Your New Home

MADE ESPECIALLY
FOR YOU BY:

Home Sweet Home

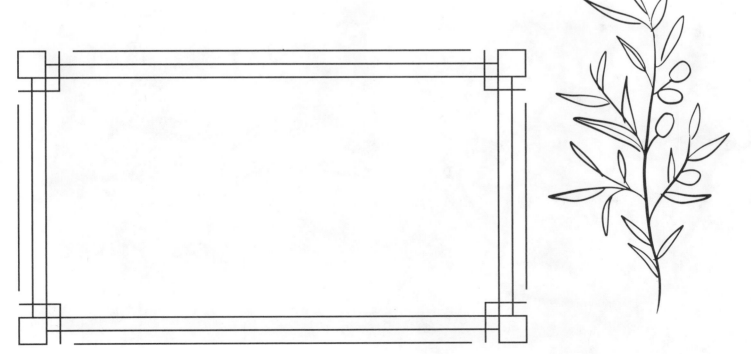

Home Sweet Home

Made with love by

For Your New Home

FOR:

MADE BY:

DATE:

Congratulations GRADUATE

CLASS OF

CLASS OF

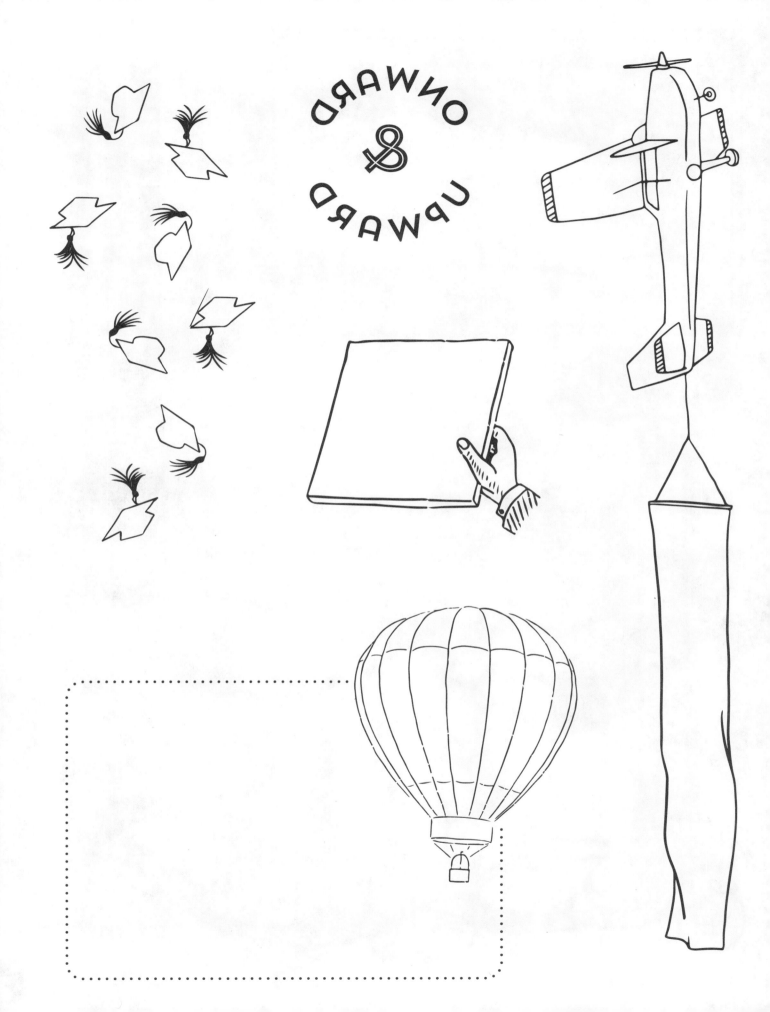

For Your Adventures

STARTS NOW
YOUR OWN
TRAVEL ON
TO KEEP YOU

For Your Adventures

TO KEEP YOU WARM ON YOUR TRAVELS

LEAVE THE ROAD.
TAKE THE TRAILS.

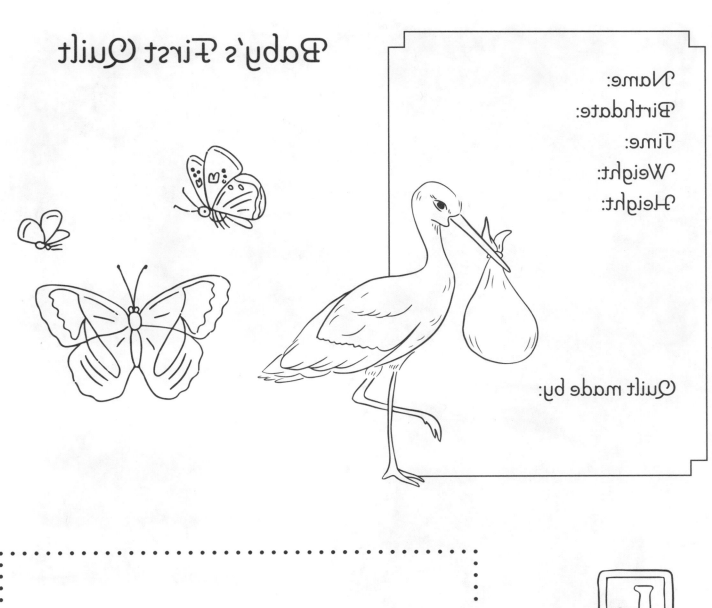

Baby's First Quilt

Name:

Birthdate:

Time:

Weight:

Height:

Quilt made by:

LOVE

Name

Birthdate

Time

Weight

Height

Quilt made by

Baby's First Quilt

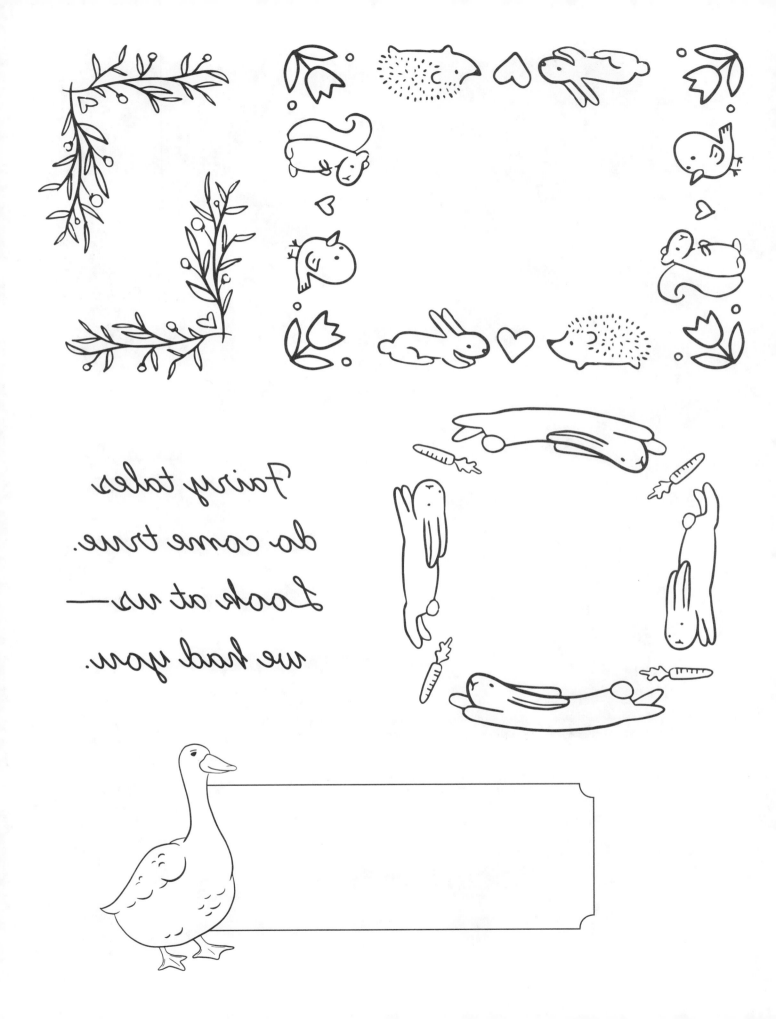

Fairy tales
do come true.
Look at us—
we had you.

For your
Little One

Sweet Dreams

Made especially for:

Made especially for

FOR MY LIL' SPROUT

Sweet Pea

FOR MY LIL SPROUT

Sweet Pea

Wishing you
a lifetime of
happiness

Made with
Love by

Happily ever after

Forever and Always

Celebrating

10 Years

15 Years

20 Years

25 Years

30 Years

35 Years

40 Years

45 Years

50 Years

...and counting!

Celebrating...
10 Years
15 Years
20 Years
25 Years
30 Years

35 Years
40 Years
45 Years
50 Years
and counting!

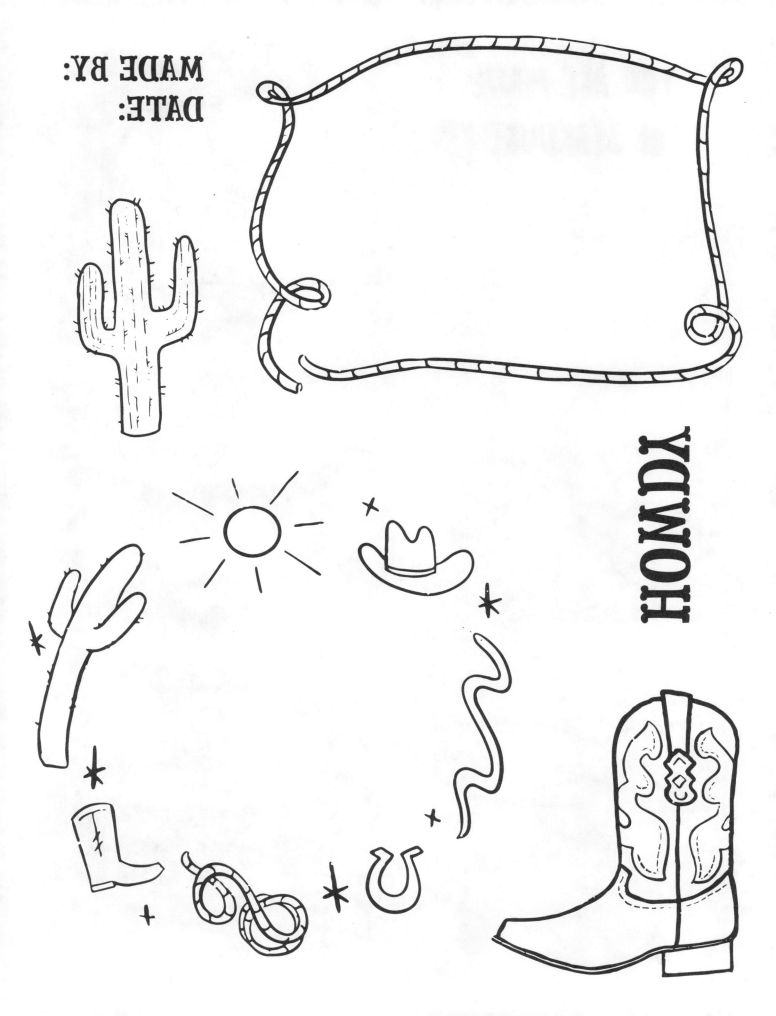

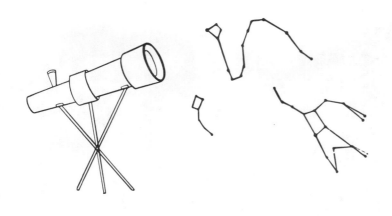

I BELIEVE IN YOU

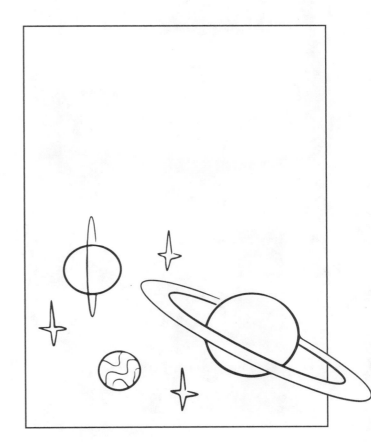

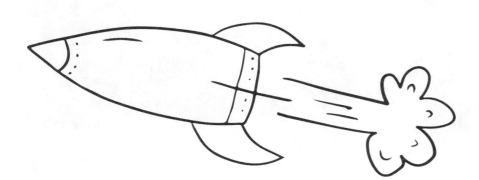

YOU ARE MADE
OF STARDUST

I BELIEVE IN YOU

Once Upon a Time

YOU ARE
THE HERO OF
YOUR STORY

You are magic

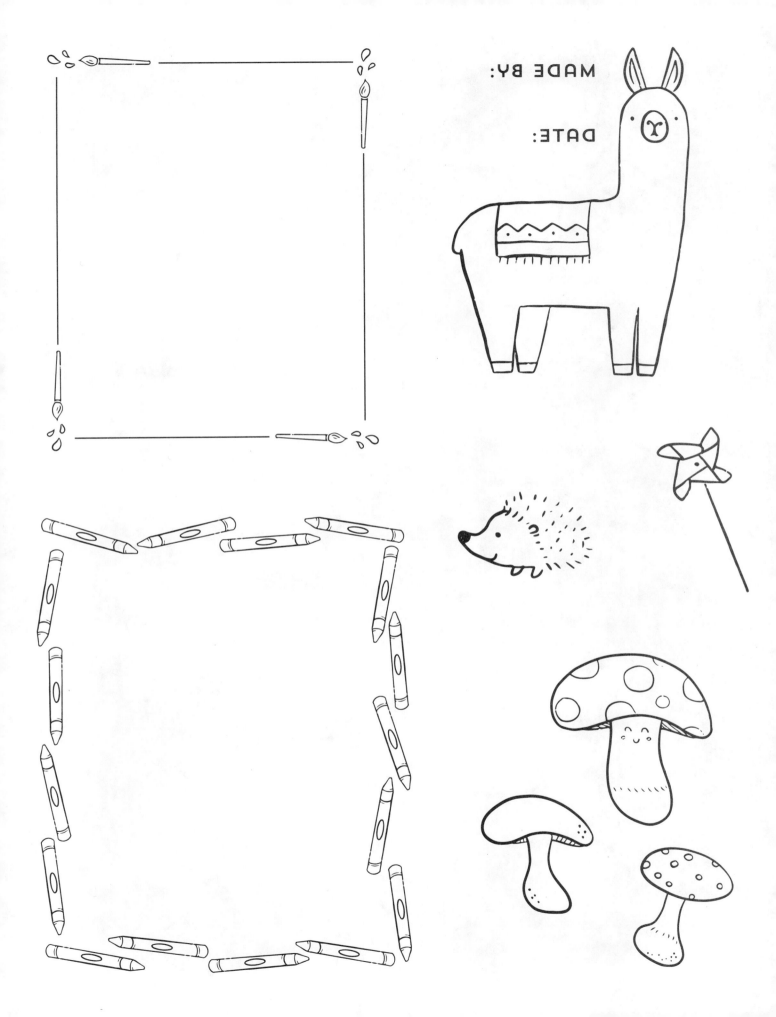

MADE BY:

DATE:

MADE BY:

DATE:

MADE WITH LOVE
FOR A RAWR-SOME KID

TEAM
MADE WITH LOVE
FOR A RAWR-SOME KID

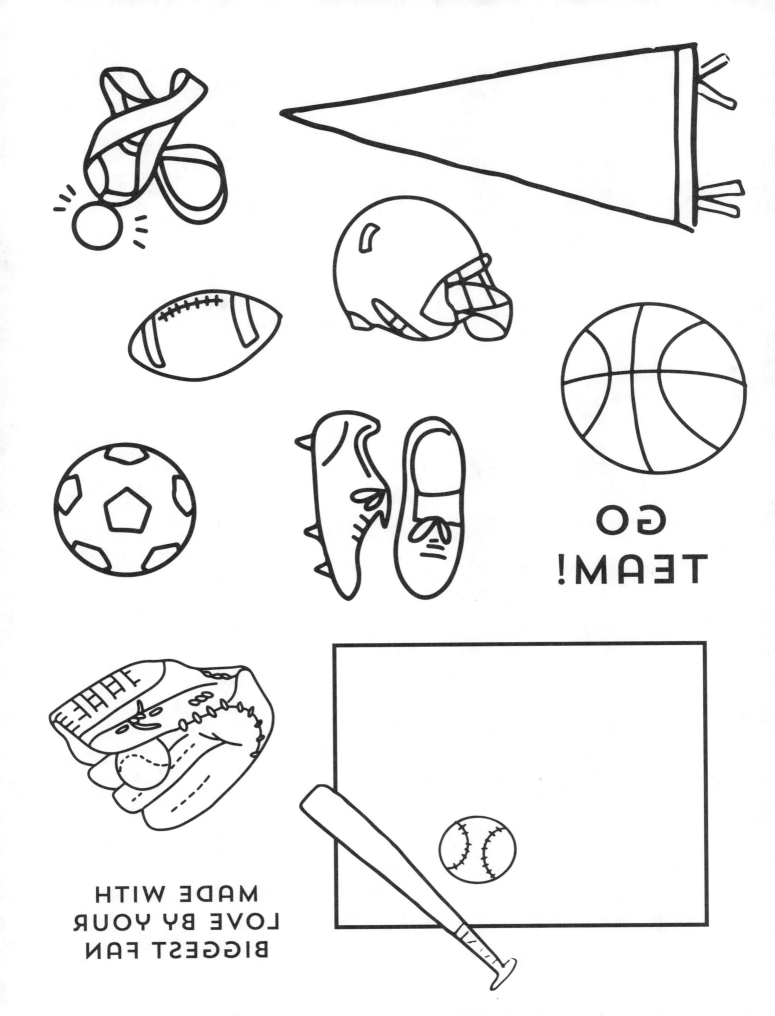

GO
TEAM!

MADE WITH
LOVE BY YOUR
BIGGEST FAN

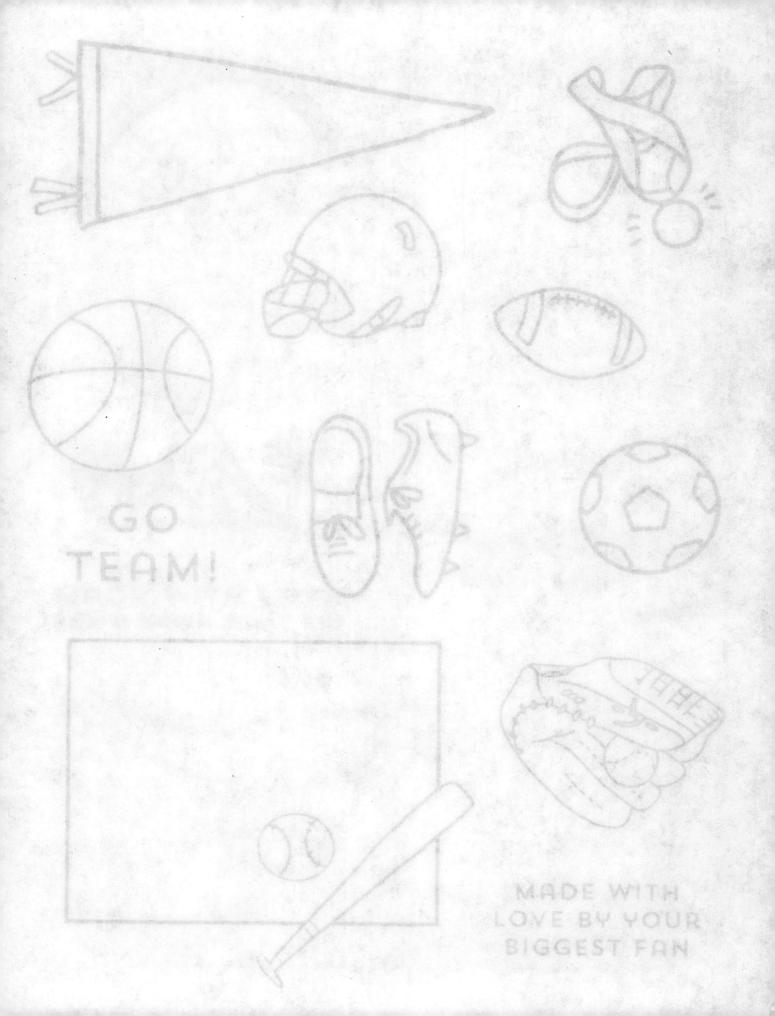

GO
TEAM!

MADE WITH
LOVE BY YOUR
BIGGEST FAN